*Avoid Being Hurt By
"The Church"*

HURT BY THE CHURCH

*When We Know That We Are
"The Church"*

By Frank L. Rodriguez

HURT BY THE CHURCH by Frank L. Rodriguez

LionofJudah520@gmail.com

All rights reserved. No part of this book may be reproduced, stored in a retrieval system, or transmitted in any form or by any means – electronic, mechanical, photocopy, recording, or otherwise – without prior written permission of the copyright owner, except as provided by United States of America copyright law.

Scripture quotations are from the New King James Version of the Bible.

Copyright © 2024 by Frank Lincoln Rodriguez
All Rights Reserved.

Editor: Naomi Rodriguez

International Standard Book Number: 9780998713175

First edition

CONTENTS

1. Growing Up In The Wilderness 9

2. Temptation of the Flesh (The Emotion) 13

3. Temptation of the Eyes (The Heart) 19

4. The Pride of Life (The Mind) 27

5. Accepting Our Humanity 33

6. The Love of The Church 35

7. The Laborers Are Few 43

8. Hurt By The Church 47

Preface

Recently I participated in a Christian home group meeting and the power and presence of God was quite evident. How?

Like some church services I have attended where there was a timely word, gifts of the Spirit in operation, and people being healed by the power of God.

Jesus was in the room.

And just as much as *some* churches condemn these individuals for having church apart from the church, there are also *some* groups that condemn the church for being "The Church."

But what is the real issue when it comes to these matters?

Because John the Baptist was in the wilderness speaking to individuals about <u>the kingdom of God</u> who were outside of the synagogue (church).

While Jesus was in the synagogues displaying the very things that John the Baptist was preaching about <u>the kingdom of God</u>.

And what exactly is the kingdom?

The Bible tells us that the kingdom of God is in you (Luke 17:21). How?

The kingdom of God has to do with *righteousness,* which is a condition of the <u>mind</u>; *peace* is the condition of the <u>heart</u>; and *joy* is an <u>emotional</u> condition; all in partnership with the Holy Spirit (Romans 14:17).

Therefore, the kingdom of God has to do with the condition of the spirit of man's soul in relationship to the Spirit of God and His soul (Hebrews 10:38).

So, is it that the people who have left the church are actually in search for the kingdom of God in the people of God; while being accused of doing "*their own thing*"?

And that is the irony of it all and the purpose as to why this book has been written.

It is coming to the understanding and recognizing whenever any of us are tempted to do our own thing, for the sake of the kingdom, in the name of Jesus Christ.

Chapter 1

Growing Up In The Wilderness

When Jesus was baptized, the Bible tells us that the Holy Spirit led Him into the wilderness. Why? It was for the same reasons the LORD God led all of Israel out into the wilderness.

It was to humble them and to test them to see if they would do what the LORD God told them to do (Deuteronomy 8:2).

So when Jesus the Son of Man was in the wilderness for 40 days, compared to the Israelites who were in the wilderness for 40 years, there was a complete and total dependency and reliance upon our all sufficient, God.

And in this dependency upon God, it requires that we become dependent upon His Word and what He is saying above what we say.

Because Jesus taught us in Mark 4:15 that Satan comes to steal the Word. And by doing so it removes our reliance upon God for the purpose of us becoming self-reliant or independent of Him.

And how does the devil do that?

It is through the temptation of the soul that communicates its strong feelings through its emotion, heart, and mind.

And according to 1 John 2:16, this is known as the lust or strong feelings of the flesh (<u>emotion</u>), lust or strong feelings of the eyes (<u>heart</u>), and the prideful feeling of the <u>mind</u>.

But the power to choose what the Spirit of the Lord is saying, above what the spirit of the soul may be saying during times of temptation, is the strength of the soul's <u>will</u>.

Luke 22:42 – (Jesus said) *...nevertheless not My will, but Yours, be done.*

The will is the authority that we all have been given that gives us the power to choose.

Deuteronomy 30:19 – *...I have set before you life and death, blessing and cursing; therefore choose life...*

Therefore, the true conflict that we face is not with a devil during times of temptation. But our battle is actually with ourselves when it comes to making the right or righteous choice.

And as we look at Jesus' temptation in the wilderness, the temptations are in the exact order in connection with the temptation of the flesh (emotion or feelings), the heart (how we see or believe), and the pride of life (our thoughts above God's).

And how do these temptation present themselves?

They present themselves in various ways pertaining to the *things of God*.

Chapter 2

Temptation of the Flesh
(The Emotions)

Matthew 4:3 – *Now when the tempter came to Him, he said, "If You are the Son of God, command that these <u>stones</u> become <u>bread</u>."*

Stone

First of all, what does the stone exemplify? It represents the Word of God (Matthew 7:24). What kind of Word of God? The hard Words of God that even His disciples said was too difficult to receive (John 6:60).

John 6:56 – *He who eats My flesh and drinks My blood abides in Me, and I in him.*

Bread

Second of all, what does the bread exemplify? It represents the Word of God (John 6:58). What kind of Word of God? The kind that is no longer hard but becomes soft and easy enough to internalize.

So, what is being prophetically communicated having to do with the stone being changed to bread in order to feed the flesh (emotions)?

It has to do with the transforming miracle of the Word of revelation. It is a temptation that sounds like this:

"Oh, so you are a Teacher of God's Word? Then tell me something that I haven't heard already."

In other words, *prove yourself*.

But Jesus told us to beware of the yeast, or the puffing up, of the Pharisees and <u>Herod</u>.

Mark 8:15 – *Then He charged them, saying, "Take heed, beware of the leaven of the Pharisees and the leaven of Herod."*

This temptation of the stone to be transformed to bread is the puffing up of Herod.

Because Herod was the type of person who *loved* to hear John the Baptist teach because it made him *feel* good.

And even though Herod would applaud the Word of God, he would never apply the Word of God.

Therefore, this temptation does not only result in feeding Herod's or the audiences flesh (emotionally), but it would also feed or stimulate the flesh of the Teacher.

It is becoming self-reliant to satisfy that part of the soul's emotional wants by using the things of God apart from God's will.

But what is the answer?

Matthew 4:4 – *But He answered and said, "It is written, 'Man shall not live by bread alone* (God's written Word), *but by every <u>word that proceeds from the mouth of God</u>.'"*

What Jesus is saying is that even though revelation of God's Word is a spiritual gift of **seeing** things anew through His written Word, we need to **hear** directly from God what we are to say or not to say when it comes to sharing *His* revelation and not ours.

It is being led by the Spirit of God and not by the spirit of our emotions in those particular moments when all are *feeling* good.

And that is why the true proving is not proving ourselves, but letting the LORD God prove us (Deut. 8:2).

And how do we know we are proved of God? When we no longer have a need to seek the *approval* of man.

For when Jesus was baptized prior to being led into the wilderness to be proven, the LORD God announced Him.

Therefore, Jesus didn't have a need nor did He have a want to announce, show or prove Himself of who He was – The Teacher (Rabbi).

<u>Notice</u>: *It is being emotionally secure in who you are in Christ.*

Chapter 3

Temptation of the Eyes
(The Heart)

Matthew 4:5-6 – *Then the devil took Him up into the holy city, set Him on the pinnacle of the temple, and said to Him, "If You are the Son of God, throw Yourself down. For it is written...etc."*

The place that the devil took Jesus was in the midst of all things pertaining to God.

And in order for Jesus to *prove Himself* of being of God according to Satan's temptation, the request was to perform the Word of God. How? Like a performer, using miracles, signs and wonders.

But again, Jesus told us to beware of the yeast or puffing up of the <u>Pharisees</u> and Herod (Mark 8:15).

Now the Pharisees were always looking for a sign. And what is interesting about a sign, like all signs, it is saying something. A sign is what gives us direction in the way to go.

But like Herod who wouldn't apply what he **heard**, the Pharisees wouldn't apply what they would **see**. They just liked to be entertained or wowed with signs.

And like the gift of a Prophet who is like a sign that says something in order to give direction, we can fall into that same temptation of, "You say that you are a prophet of God, then prophecy."

In other words, read my mail so I can *see* it for myself and maybe then I'll believe it in my *heart* that you truly are from God.

And then there is also the temptation of, "You say that you are a prophet of God. Then what have you prophesied that has come to pass?"

As the Prophet mistakenly goes on speaking of past prophesies into the hearts of individuals who are too blind to *see* what the Lord is saying from these prophetic signs coming from His *heart*.

As a result of falling for these kinds of temptations, they are now serving the kingdom of darkness as its Court Jester (entertainer), rather than being a servant in the Courts of God's Kingdom as His Prophet.

And why does this happen?

It is the audiences desire for the gift, and the Prophet's appreciation of his or her gift, that loses direction for the desire and appreciation of the gift Giver – God Himself.

They just all *love* prophecy.

And the reason why some people love prophecy is because the gift of prophecy edifies, exhorts and comforts. It is a gift that can satisfy the lust or strong desire of a *heart* that is actually insecure.

And that insecure individual can be the recipient of the prophecy as well as the Prophet themselves.

Deuteronomy 8:2 – *"And you shall remember that the LORD your God led you these forty years in the wilderness, to humble you and test you, to know what was in your heart, whether you would keep His commandments or not.*

Therefore, the answer to this particular temptation when it comes to prophecy is that we no longer put the LORD God to the test (Matthew 4:7).

Matthew 4:7 – *Jesus said to him, "It is written again, 'You shall not tempt the LORD your God'."*

It is having the confidence in knowing in our *heart* the personal relationship we have with the Father's loving acceptance of us apart from the gift.

And as a result, it will not permit the temptation for us to be tested with the gift. How?

It is no longer looking to be accepted by man, when we know that we are accepted by the Father for who we are and not for what we do.

Notice: It is having a heart for God's loving acceptance that is found in Christ.

A Prophetic Summary:

Abraham Overcame His Temptation

When the Lord told Abraham to let Ishmael go, it represented the physical gift (*flesh or emotion*).

And when the Lord told Abraham to sacrifice Isaac, it represented the spiritual gift (*heart*).

And why sacrifice the gifts that can be the result of a *heart* condition?

It is for the sake of the greatest gift of all which is love - God Himself.

For instance, it can be falling in love with the person of God as Father. And not falling in love with what Father has in His pockets that He may gift us that then makes us feel good (a revelation gift, a personal prophecy, offerings, ...etc.).

Otherwise it is coming to a loving Father not for who He <u>is</u>, but rather loving on Him for what He <u>does</u> (works).

And that alone is the very essence of having conditional love for an unconditional loving Father.

John 21:15 – *…Jesus said to Simon Peter* (the Church), *"Simon, son of Jonah, do you love Me more than these* (people)*?"*

Chapter 4

The Pride of Life
(The Mind)

Matthew 4:8-9 – *Again, the devil took Him up on an exceedingly high mountain, and showed Him all the kingdoms of the world and their glory. And he said to Him, "All these things I will give You if You will fall down and worship me."*

The Apostle – the kingdom builders.

Jesus said that He came to establish His kingdom, and kingdom influence is when heaven impacts earth.

Therefore, this is a calling of God upon the life of an individual who is very influential that can make a difference.

And as we can see, the location of the temptation took Jesus at the top of a mountain. Why?

Apostles are individuals who can usually see the big picture above the rest because of having a heavenly point of view that comes with the gift.

But this mountain of *pride* that Satan took Jesus to can tempt an apostle to get into their *mind* to see how they can possibly use their influential gift to accomplish their calling.

This is when 'the ministry' becomes more important than 'the mission' that becomes a part of their glory. And why does this happen?

It comes from spending much time in the valley.

The temptation can become the result of waiting a long time for the promises of God to finally come to pass. And as a result, there is a desire to help God by helping themselves.

Time In The Valley

1 Corinthians 4:9-14 – *For I think that God has displayed us, the <u>apostles, last,</u> as men condemned to death; for we have been made a spectacle to the world, both to angels and to men. We are fools for Christ's sake, but you are wise in Christ! We are weak, but you are strong! You are distinguished, but we are dishonored. To the present hour we both hunger and thirst, and we are poorly clothed, and beaten, and homeless. And we labor, working with our hands. Being reviled, we bless; being persecuted, we endure; being defamed, we entreat. We have been made as the filth of the world, the offscouring of all things until now. I do not write these things to shame you, but as my beloved children I warn you.*

Apostles pay a heavy price for being a foundation that will carry the weight of God's glory without having to take any glory for them selves (Ephesians 2:20).

But the temptation has to do with not being moved with compassion for the people (Matthew 14:14), but rather being motivated with a passion to work the gift. How? Not based on the vision but theirs according to *their* point of view.

So what did Jesus say is the answer?

Matthew 4:10 – *Then Jesus said to him, "Away with you, Satan! For it is written, 'You shall worship the LORD your God, and Him only you shall serve'."*

It is not worshiping the work or the calling of God but first worshipping the LORD and serving Him, and all these *things* will be added (Matthew 6:33).

Notice: *It is having a confidence in knowing our level of importance to the Father that will not permit us to devalue our sense of significance by doing something outside of His honor for the sake of our own.*

Chapter 5

Accepting Our Humanity

When it comes to the emotion, heart and mind of all mankind, we all need security, acceptance and a sense of significance or importance.

And when we do these things for ourselves through the spirit of the soul in the name of God, it becomes self-glorifying.

But when we come to know and accept how secure, accepted, and significant we are in the love of God from God, that is when His glory shines upon us. And when it does, we don't need to take care of those needs of the soul through the souls of others.

1 Peter 2:25 – *For you were like sheep going astray, but have now returned to* *the Shepherd and Overseer of your souls.*

That is why the Holy Spirit is known as the Comforter. We become comfortable and not unsure or insecure of being who we are in Him. And this was a major part of the original temptation.

Matthew 4:3 & 6 – *"If You are the Son of God…etc."*

Therefore, the summary of all these temptations that have everything to do with God and His Word, gifts, worship, and serving is loving the <u>person</u> of God above loving the <u>things</u> of God.

<u>***Notice:***</u> ***We are not what we do, but we are whose we are – a son and daughter of the Most High.***

Chapter 6

The Love of The Church

1 Corinthians 12:28 – *And God has appointed these in the church: <u>first</u> apostles, second prophets, third teachers…*

As we can see, this scripture is setting in order God's church based on its function and its level of influence for the sake of its wellbeing.

And even though we have rightly made each a position in the Church, we never need to endeavor the kinds of gifts that come with these administrations in order to attain them or its position. Why?

Because a person is simply created with a gift, as the gift, as they learn to perfect or mature themselves in the gift (Ephesians 1:1).

Galatians 1:15 – *But when it pleased God, who separated me from my mother's womb and called me through His grace,*

That said, there could be prophets that may not know they are prophets until they come to know Jesus.

And then there are apostles (leaders of influence and visionaries) who are apostles whether they are in the church or outside of the Church (1 Corinthians 12:28).

Then there are great teachers who may not necessarily be teachers of the gospel that are known as teacher, trainer, instructor, professor...etc. They simply are who and what they are.

1 Corinthians 15:10 – *But by the grace of God I am what I am...*

And how are the Apostles, Prophets, and Teachers most effective in their gift based on their level of influence? We find the answer in the love Chapter of the Bible.

It is where the Apostle Paul is actually speaking to the Teachers, the Prophets, and the Apostles *first*.

Teacher

1 Corinthians 13:1 – *Though I speak* (teach) *with tongues of men* (relative understanding) *and angels* (heavenly revelation), *but have not love, I have become <u>sounding brass or a clanging cymbal</u>.*

When a teacher can teach as the Apostle Paul did to get certain individuals to understand either basic concepts (tongues of men) or revelatory insight (tongues of angels), it relies highly on being in touch with the Spirit. Because the Spirit knows how to reach an individual based on their spiritual condition.

And yet this oratory gift like a musical instrument can become something that is out of tone, out of time, and out of tune with the harmonies of heaven.

And as a result, it is out of reach with the people of God.

Because being out of touch with what God's Spirit desires to communicate or not communicate no longer serves the people, but becomes self-serving where the people are at a loss.

As the scripture says, it is like the sounding brass (crashing gong) or cymbal player in an orchestra. And a true instrument of heaven possesses enough self-control to know when it is time to bring in the right sound.

But a person that no longer has an ear to hear what the Spirit is saying to the Church is actually out of touch with what the Spirit in saying.

Therefore, a person can go on and on and on taking pleasure with their performance based on their knowledge of God's Word (Yeast of Herod), while losing the audiences ability to understand a word that they are saying.

These are the applause but without application. These are times of preaching a *good word* but not a *God word* that can affect real change.

Prophet

1 Corinthians 13:2 – *And though I have the gift of prophecy, and understand all mysteries and all knowledge, and though I have all faith,* *so that I could remove mountains, but have not love, <u>I am nothing</u>.*

Why is it that they are nothing without love? It is because of the gift they think that they are something special (Yeast of the Pharisees).

Apostle

1 Corinthians 13:3 – *And though I bestow all my goods to feed the poor, and though I give my body to be burned, but have not love, <u>it profits me nothing</u>.*

First of all, the price of an apostle is great. And being as an influential individual can result in the kind of temptation that desires to gain at the expense of others. In what way?

As mentioned earlier, an apostle is as a foundation, which is something that usually goes unnoticed and unrecognized. It is the price they are required to pay to become what God has called them to be.

Therefore, the objective in their giving of themselves can become tainted with the temptation to want something in return.

Whether it may be some form of recognition or compensation, it becomes self-serving that in the end profits them nothing.

Matthew 6:1 – *"Take heed that you do not do your charitable deeds before men, to be seen by them. Otherwise you have no reward from your Father in heaven."*

As I mentioned before, it is becoming ministry minded rather than mission minded when the focus has been removed from the true purpose – all in the name of Christ.

Because even though the devil tried to tempt Jesus by flawlessly quoting the Word of God (Matthew 4:6), what was it that made it so wrong?

It was the spirit, which is the true intent and purpose of the heart.

John 4:23 – *But the hour is coming, and now is, when the true worshipers will worship the Father in spirit and in truth* (complete honesty); *for the Father is seeking such to worship Him.*

Chapter 7

The Laborers Are Few

Matthew 9:37-38 – *Then He said to His disciples, "The harvest truly is plentiful, but the laborers are few. Therefore pray the Lord of the harvest to send out laborers into His harvest."*

In Luke 9:1, Jesus gave His disciples *all* power to cast out devils and heal the sick.

But when the disciples had all power to do just that, it got to the point where they couldn't cast out this one that was in a child (Luke 9:37-42). Why?

They were now doing what Jesus did but with no power because they lost their innocent child-like faith. How?

By behaving childishly, as they began comparing themselves with one another (Luke 9:46-47).

Therefore, you cannot cast out a demon that is from pride with pride.

In the end, it is doing all the right things pertaining to God, but with the wrong spirit (intent and purpose).

No power! But be not deceived.

For even God permitted the miracle of the water to come forth from the rock in the midst of Moses' disobedience.

And that is because God cares more about meeting the needs of the people, than the want(s) of the person.

Consequently give and it shall be given is a spiritual principle that says deceive and you will become deceived. And what I believe to be the worst deception is self-deception (2 Timothy 3:13).

So after Jesus sent out the twelve disciples, upon their return He now appoints seventy to go out and do the work of the ministry (Luke 10:1).

And as they all returned, they rejoiced over the ability to do those things like Jesus did by casting out demons (Luke 10:17).

But Jesus told them not to rejoice over those things but to rejoice that their names were written in heaven. Why?

It's better than having their names being written in lights that will eventually go down in history.

Because when Jesus casted a demon out from an individual, it would not only draw the crowd, but His popularity grew throughout the entire region (Mark 5:1-17).

Therefore the laborers that are few, does not mean that there aren't enough people preaching Jesus. But the laborers that are few are the few who have worked out their own salvation of the soul *first*.

And that is the true work of a person's ministry, which is the ministry of reconciliation.

It is when we reconcile the spirit of our soul in agreement with the Spirit of God's (2 Corinthians 5:18).

It's agreeing to do God's will God's way.

Deuteronomy 8:2 – *"And you shall remember that the LORD your God led you all the way these forty years in the wilderness, to humble you…*

Chapter 8

Hurt By The Church

So, who is "the Church?"

Referring to the Church as its own entity is like people who want to blame "the Government."

And as long as we just see it as a whole, there is no true accountability on any*one's* part that can make a difference.

In the end, it will only produce the same result that produces the same argument.

And so who is this group, no matter what kind of group it is, whether it is large or small? Whether it is in a church setting or in a home group meeting?

They are made up of persons. What kind of persons or people?

They are people just like all of us who may have a title or may not have a title as an apostle or leader, prophet or director, teacher or instructor that have the power to make a difference.

And yet, they are all individuals created with needs of the soul as we all have been as it pertains to security, acceptance, and significance.

And that is why the Bible tells us to pray for our leaders. What leaders? All leaders when it comes to the church and those outside of the church; which includes those in government.

1 Timothy 2:1-2 – *Therefore I exhort first of all that supplications, prayers, intercessions, and giving of thanks be made for all men, for kings and all who* *are in authority, that we may lead a quiet and peaceable life in all godliness and reverence.*

And as a result, we will live in peace, godliness, and reverence not for what others do or don't do, but what we are doing by praying in the Spirit with understanding (1 Corinthians 14:15). Understanding what?

Understanding that we all need help regarding these matters of the soul.

Because we all need God's help when it comes to taking care of His business (people) without having a desire to want to take care of our own (person) at their expense.

And that pertains to the Church, those outside the church, those in government...etc.

Psalm 23:1 – *The LORD is my shepherd; I shall not (be in) want.*

Therefore, the responsibility that we all have is first and foremost to God.

And how are we to do that? By having a love that forgives. And we begin by forgiving ourselves.

We forgive ourselves for the times when we sought out our own glory through God's people based on what we knew more than them; what gifts we had that they didn't; and the influence we may have had on them that they were not aware of.

It is because a person who knows more than another person can typically control a conversation (teacher, prophets, apostle).

But a person who knows another person better than they know

themselves can control them (applause, approval, recognition).

Therefore, we need to love others as we love ourselves by also forgiving people for being the people that they are. The kind that came short of the glory of God as they sought their own in the name of God. How?

Like we all once did, and are now tempted to do, and have the potential of doing in the future whenever these various kinds of temptations present themselves.

Because even though a person is tempted, it does not mean that they are in sin (Hebrews 4:15). It means that they are human.

Therefore, the Bible says that we mature by going from glory to glory (2 Corinthians 3:18); that transcends through a faith that continues to grow in faith (Romans 1:17); that can only work by love (Galatians 5:6).

And this is what the Apostle Peter has to say regarding all these matters:

1 Peter 2:1 – *Therefore, laying aside all malice* (hard feelings), *all deceit* (manipulation), *hypocrisy* (falsehood), *envy* (desiring to be something special) *and all evil speaking* (by putting others down to build oneself up).

According to 1 Peter 2:1, it's getting away from the conversation regarding *'those people'*, whether they are those in "the Church", outside the church, or in government who can become guilty of doing "*their own thing.*"

1 Peter 2:2 – *as newborn babes* (who are innocent), *desire the pure milk of the word, that you may grow thereby* (in respect to the salvation of our own soul),

Basically speaking, it is making our human complexities simplistic by making life in Christ Jesus as simple as possible. How?

Revelation 2:2-4 – *...I know your works* (prophet), *your labor* (teacher), *your patience* (apostle), *and that you cannot bear those who are evil. And you have tested those who say they are apostles* (leaders) *and are not, and have found them liars; and you have persevered and have patience, and have labored for My name's sake and have not become weary. Nevertheless I have this against you, that you have left your **first** love.*

Loving God above the things of God is the greatest gift and calling of all (1 Corinthians 13:13).

www.ingramcontent.com/pod-product-compliance
Lightning Source LLC
Chambersburg PA
CBHW070501050426
42449CB00012B/3075